Table of Contents

Introduction by Morris I. Leibman, Esq. vii

Biographical Sketches of Participants ix

Opening Remarks by Leonard J. Theberge, Esq.
and Dr. Yonah Alexander 1

Panel One: Domestic Experience
1. Morris I. Leibman, Esq., Moderator 5
2. Senator Jeremiah A. Denton 6
3. Charles Fenyvesi 12
4. Wayne R. Gilbert 14
5. Eugene H. Methvin 16
6. The Honorable Frank H. Perez 19
7. Ford Rowan, Esq. 21
8. George Watson 25
9. Questions from the Audience 28

Panel Two: Overseas Experience
1. Dr. John McLaughlin, Moderator 35
2. The Honorable Diego C. Asencio 36
3. Dr. W. Scott Thompson 38
4. Nicholas Ashford 41
5. Ali Birand 45
6. Marino de Medici 47
7. Shalom Kital 50
8. Dr. Dieter Kronzucker 51

Table of Contents (Continued)

9. Questions from the Audience 53
Concluding Remarks: William Claire 61
Appendix: Statistical Overview of Terrorist Incidents 63
Type of Victim of International Terrorist Incidents,
1982 and 1983 63
Category of International Terrorist Incidents,
1982 and 1983 63
Geographic Distribution of Terrorist Incidents,
1982 and 1983 64
Geographic Distribution of International Terrorist
Incidents, 1981, by Category 65

TERRORISM AND THE MEDIA IN THE 1980's

With an Introduction
by Morris I. Leibman, Esq.

The proceedings of a conference held April 14, 1983
Cosponsored by
Transnational Communications Center, The Media Institute
and
Institute for Studies in International Terrorism,
State University of New York

Edited by Sarah Midgley
and Virginia Rice

Transnational Communications Center
The Media Institute
Washington, D.C.

Copyright (c) 1984 The Media Institute

All rights reserved. No part of this publication may be reproduced or transmitted in any form without permission in writing from the publisher.

First printing March 1984.

Published by The Media Institute, Washington, D.C.

Printed in the United States of America.

ISBN: 0-937790-26-5

Library of Congress Catalog Card Number: 84-70399

Introduction

The purpose of this seminar on terrorism and the media was to discuss the relationship between news coverage and terrorist events. It gave the panelists the opportunity to share their views on the seriousness of the world terrorist movement and to evaluate the need for well-conceived guidelines to deal with terrorist acts as they occur. Some of the aspects discussed were the extent of exploitation of the media by terrorists, whether or not boundaries of legitimate coverage should be established and whether self-restraint can be imposed or if formal legislation is needed.

This program, sponsored by The Media Institute's Transnational Communications Center and The Institute for Studies in International Terrorism at the State University of New York, also explored in depth the symbiotic relationship between the media and the terrorist. As one panelist aptly put it, "Terrorism is an act of theater, the media is its stage". Terrorist acts have become media events -- they do not achieve their end unless given publicity.

The issue of terrorism, of course, cuts across that all too-fine-line between the cherished ideal of free speech and censorship. Terrorism has now become a political problem. Among today's leaders are former terrorists. Curbing media coverage of such events could be construed as a form of censorship. But there also lies the inherent danger that too little or too much coverage could act as a catalyst in escalating the number and seriousness of the acts. We need to consider a balance between keeping the people informed, panic publicity, and real questions of public security.

Many experts in this field propose guidelines such as those used at CBS. These internal restraints would leave the media responsible for policing its own actions and using its judgment as to what extent coverage will be given to each terrorist act. Others feel, however, that the media, by virtue of its very nature, will not be firm enough and suggest that formal legislation is necessary to keep the media in hand. There is strong support for the position that the public's right to know is secondary to the safety of the people involved. A consensus, so far, has not been reached.

For myself, I would suggest that the real danger facing the free world today is underestimating the total across-the-board war that is being waged against our society. Terrorism, assasinations, and guerilla warfare are tools being used to achieve definite ends. We need to understand that terrorism is now accepted by our enemies as a specialized profession and is being interwoven with propaganda and disinformation as part of the war for the minds of men and women. Because the media is news-oriented rather than issue-oriented, analysis of these all-encompassing communication attacks is often lacking. We need to develop new understanding, skills and abilities to cope with this new assault on freedom's terrain. This program, we hope, will play a small, but vital part in starting this much-needed development process.

Morris I. Leibman

Chicago
February 1984

Biographical Sketches of Participants

DR. YONAH ALEXANDER

Yonah Alexander is Director and Professor at the Institute for Studies in International Terrorism, State University of New York. He is also a Senior Staff Member at the Center for Strategic and International Studies, Georgetown University, and a Fellow at the Institute for Social and Behavioral Pathology, University of Chicago. Dr. Alexander is Editor-in-Chief of Terrorism: An International Journal and Political Communication and Persuasion: An International Journal. He has authored, edited and co-edited over twenty books.

THE HONORABLE DIEGO C. ASENCIO

Ambassador Diego Asencio is the Assistant Secretary of State for Consular Affairs. He is a career Foreign Service Officer who served as U.S. Ambassador to Colombia from 1977 to 1980. His other assignments have included Deputy Chief of Mission in Venezuela and Portugal, Political Officer in Panama, and Protection and Welfare Officer in Mexico. In 1980 Ambassador Asencio was taken hostage in Colombia by a group of political terrorists. He was released after 61 days and was later awarded the Department of State's Award for Valor and the President's Award of the American Society for Public Administration.

NICHOLAS ASHFORD

Nicholas Ashford is Bureau Chief of the Washington bureau of The Times (London). After beginning his journalism career with the London Financial Times, he joined The Times in 1969 and has served as a foreign correspondent in the Middle East, Europe and southern Africa. He has broadcast extensively with BBC and French radio and has written numerous articles for other publications on the Middle East and Southern Africa.

ALI BIRAND

Ali Birand is the Washington correspondent for Milliyet, of Istanbul, Turkey.

WILLIAM CLAIRE

William Claire is the former Director of the Washington Office of the State University of New York, the largest public university system in America, consisting of 64 separate campuses. In addition to having written six books and numerous articles in both national and international journals, Mr. Claire was founding Editor and Publisher of Voyage, an award-winning literary magazine. He is a graduate of Georgetown and Columbia Universities.

MARINO DE MEDICI

Marino de Medici has been the U.S. Correspondent for Il Tempo for 15 years and is a contributor to numerous newspapers and magazines. He is a graduate of the University of Washington in Seattle and received his M.A. from the University of California in Berkeley.

SENATOR JEREMIAH A. DENTON

Senator Denton (R-AL) is Chairman of the Subcommittee on Security and Terrorism, Committee on the Judiciary. He is also a member of the Labor and Human Resources and Veterans Affairs Committees. Prior to beginning his political career, Denton served in the U.S. Navy for 31 years and achieved the rank of Rear Admiral. He is author of When Hell Was in Session, a book about the 7 1/2 years he spent as a North Vietnamese POW. Senator Denton was named Man of the Year by Morality in Media (1977) and Citizens for Decency through Law (1976).

CHARLES FENYVESI

Charles Fenyvesi is Editor of Washington Jewish Week and Garden Columnist for The Washington Post. He is also a free lance writer whose articles have appeared in New Republic and The Washington Post. In 1977 Mr. Fenyvesi was one of the hostages taken by Hanafi Muslims at the B'nai B'rith building in Washington.

WAYNE R. GILBERT

Wayne Gilbert is Deputy Assistant Director of the Criminal Investigative Division of the FBI. A graduate of the University of Massachusetts in Amherst, Mr. Gilbert has served in the FBI since 1965 in a variety of positions which have included Assistant Special Agent in Oklahoma City, Inspector in the Inspection Division, and Chief of the Personal and Property Crimes Section.

SHALOM KITAL

Shalom Kital is the Washington correspondent for the Israeli Broadcasting Authority.

DR. DIETER KRONZUCKER

Dieter Kronzucker has been the Washington correspondent for ZDF German Television since 1981. His previous positions have included Anchorman of "Heute-Journal," a daily news magazine of ZDF German Television in Wiesbaden, and Director of "Weltspiegel," a foreign news program of ARD German Television in Hamburg. Dr. Kronzucker has been in the film and television industry for 20 years and has been a correspondent in Vietnam, Spain and Latin America.

MORRIS I. LEIBMAN, Esq.

Morris Leibman, a partner of Sidley & Austin in Chicago, is the former Chairman of the American Bar Association's Standing Committee on Law and National Security and a member of the Executive Board of Georgetown University's Center for Strategic and International Studies. A graduate of University of Chicago Law School, Mr. Leibman has lectured extensively on domestic and international affairs and was awarded the Presidential Medal of Freedom by President Reagan in 1981. He is also a Director of the National Strategy Information Center (New York City) and The Foreign Policy Research Institute (Philadelphia).

DR. JOHN McLAUGHLIN

John McLaughlin is Moderator of "The McLaughlin Group," a weekly NBC discussion program which deals with a full range of domestic and international public policy issues. In addition, Dr. McLaughlin is Executive Editor (Washington) of The National Review, as well as Commentator on National Public Radio and the NBC radio network. Prior to his present positions, he served as Special Assistant to former U.S. Presidents Gerald Ford and Richard Nixon.

Throughout his career he has travelled extensively to Latin America, Africa and the Middle East.

EUGENE H. METHVIN

Eugene Methvin is a Senior Editor of Reader's Digest and the author of The Riot Makers: The Technology of Social Demolition and The Rise of Radicalism. He has written articles on a variety of topics ranging from civil liberties and constitutional law to terrorism and U.S.-Soviet relations. He is past President of the Washington Professional Chapter of the Society of Professional Journalists and is former Director of the Foreign Policy Research Institution.

THE HONORABLE FRANK H. PEREZ

Frank Perez is Deputy Chief of Mission in Ankara, Turkey. He was formerly Deputy Director of the Office for Combatting Terrorism, U.S. Department of State. Previously he was Deputy U.S. Representative to the Strategic Arms Talks in Geneva. A graduate of the National War College, Mr. Perez is a career Foreign Service Officer whose other positions have included Political Advisor to the U.S. Mission to NATO, Member of the Secretary's Policy Planning Staff, and Director of the Office of Strategic and General Research.

FORD ROWAN, Esq.

Ford Rowan is Host of the new Public Broadcasting System's series, "International Edition," and a Senior Washington Correspondent for "Independent Network News," a nightly news program carried by 40 television stations. A former NBC News reporter, Rowan is Resident Counsel in Washington for the North Carolina law firm Sanford, Adams, McCullough & Beard. He specializes in communications and First Amendment law.

LEONARD J. THEBERGE, Esq.

Leonard J. Theberge was President of The Media Institute until his death in October 1983. He authored and edited numerous articles and books on multinational corporations, international communications, and business-media relations. In 1975 he founded and served as President of the National Legal Center for the Public Interest. He was past Chairman of the American Bar Association's Section of International Law and Practice and Chairman of the Section's International Communications Committee. He was a Trustee of the International Law Institute, a Director of the Capital Legal Foundation and President of the St. Peter's College, Oxford Foundation.

DR. W. SCOTT THOMPSON

Scott Thompson, Director of the American Security Council, was the former Associate Director for Programs at the U.S. Information Agency. Previously he was Associate Professor of International Politics at the Fletcher School of Law and Diplomacy and Adjunct Professor at Georgetown University's School of Foreign Service. Dr. Thompson received his Ph.D. from Oxford University and his B.A. from Stanford University. He is the author of eight books on Comparative Politics and International Affairs.

GEORGE WATSON

George Watson monitors the fairness and accuracy of all ABC News reports as Vice President of ABC News. He also serves as ABC News' liaison with other journalistic organizations and professional groups both in the U.S. and abroad. Prior to his present position, he was Vice President and Washington Bureau Chief of ABC News, as well as an ABC News correspondent in the United States and overseas. He has also served Cable News Network as Washington Vice President and Managing Editor.

TERRORISM AND THE MEDIA IN THE 1980's

Opening Remarks

Leonard J. Theberge, Esq.
President
The Media Institute

The panelists who have assembled here today will be examining the complex domestic and international challenge which terrorism represents. Their insights and experiences will be useful to those of you who are faced with this intractable problem. It goes without saying that the issue is extremely complicated, but we have all addressed complicated issues. Moreover, complexity should not be confused with impossibility. Today's conference will undoubtedly illuminate that complexity, but it should also enhance our understanding of the many facets which make up the relationship between terrorists and the media.

Dr. Yonah Alexander
Director
The Institute for Studies in
  International Terrorism

Contemporary terrorism is an expedient political and strategical tool for the power struggle within and among nations. It illustrates the increasing lack of distinction between a state of war and a state of peace. As we approach 1984, Orwell's famous dictum that "Peace is war" assumes a greater sense of reality. Terrorism is a form of low-intensity political conflict which falls below the threshold of a clearly recognized military operation and, as such, it is one of the most menacing methods of disrupting the fabric of civilized order in an open society. Terrorism has introduced a new breed of violence through psychological warfare and propaganda. As the communications revolution shrinks the world, terrorists are able to obtain unprecedented publicity for their deeds. The most dramatic example of the de facto terrorist-media linkage was the takeover of the U.S. Embassy in Teheran. This crisis of 444 days illustrated that terrorism, with continuous media coverage, can become a devastating political weapon with tragic implications for all concerned.

Several problems must be considered in discussing the link between terrorists and the media. First, extensive coverage by the media is a major reward for terrorists. The establishment of communications channels, willingly or unwillingly, is a tool in the terrorist strategy. Reporting on terrorism increases the effectiveness of its message through repetition and imitation.

The second point concerns the vital importance of a free press and the public's need to know. A related, critical issue is the relationship between the media and the police agencies. Although each has a duty to society and a right to perform that duty, generally acceptable guidelines for either have not been developed. The fundamental question is how the media, in a democratic society, can devise methods to report fairly on terrorist activities without abrogating their responsibility to the public and without adversely affecting the management of law enforcement agencies.

Today's conference will focus on the interaction between terrorism and the media, the complexity of the link between the two, and the seriousness of the consequences of that link. The questions which will be discussed include:

1. Do news reports cause or encourage terrorism?
2. Would terrorism decline if the media ignored or downplayed it?
3. Are there any steps which the media can take to minimize exploitation by a terrorist initiative?
4. What is the appropriate limit of the news coverage of a terrorist action?
5. Should radio and television coverage of terrorist activities be delayed?
6. Should attempts be made to deny reporters access to information during a terrorist event?
7. Is it possible to legislate boundaries of legitimate coverage of incidents?
8. Is self-censorship by the media a good idea or even possible given the competitive nature of news organizations?
9. Should self-restraint be imposed in specific areas in cases of terrorism?
10. Should the media provide full coverage of terrorism during an incident?
11. If the media does censor itself, will terrorists escalate their activities until the media simply cannot ignore them?
12. What should be the proper relationship between the media and the police agencies?

By exploring the theoretical and practical aspects of this question, we hope to increase our own and the public's knowledge of this issue, open new opportunities for investigation, stimulate an exchange of needs and concerns between the media and the law enforcement agencies, and enhance policy formulation and planning by both the media and criminal justice bodies.

Panel One: Domestic Experience

Moderator: Morris I. Leibman, Esq.
Sidley & Austin

Speaking as a lawyer, I should point out that our treatment of law and national security has developed as a new field. We never recognized national security as a major field of law. But we have learned that there is a plethora of subjects that can be taken under that heading: the Freedom of Information Act, intelligence treaties, genocide, East-West trade, the Taiwanese-Chinese issue, NATO questions, the Caribbean conflict, covert action, overt action, war-powers limitations, and so on. We are still trying to determine how our legal system would handle the General Dozier case if it happened in the United States. It is a pleasure for me to be your moderator and hear the media handle terror for a change.

Senator Jeremiah A. Denton
Chairman
Subcommittee on Security and Terrorism (Judiciary)

Terrorism has been defined as violence used to create fear. It is aimed at creating a fear which will cause other people to take action furthering the goals of the terrorist. A terrorist is always in the position of undertaking actions whose immediate physical consequences are not the same as the results which the terrorist ultimately seeks. A soldier shoots to kill an enemy. An ordinary murderer kills because he wants his victim dead. A terrorist kills people whose life or death may be a matter of complete personal indifference to him. He may do so as part of an effort to provoke increasingly brutal police repression, as attempted by terrorists in Uruguay. Claire Sterling, in her testimony before the House Subcommittee on Security and Terrorism, outlined the chain of events in that Latin American country:

> Uruguay was one of the few functioning democracies in South America. More than merely a functioning democracy, it was very proud of its freedom. It had a moderate left social democratic government at the time of the great crisis. It had the first comprehensive social welfare program in the Western Hemisphere. In short, it was--if not a model--free of a great many of the rankling grievances that may have created such difficulties in other parts of Latin America...Urban guerilla warfare tactics then began in 1970 with bombings, kidnappings, assassinations--first of Daniel Mitrione, an American official working with the anti-insurgent forces there, and then going on to assassinate more or less indiscriminately, to seize radio stations, to bomb commercial buildings, stores and automobiles, to burn houses, and so on. It became an indiscriminate attack against the civilian population. The effort was to exacerbate social tensions, to show the government as an impotent force incapable of maintaining public order, and to force it into repressive measures of response. Between 1970

and 1972, the situation became so bad that an elected parliament invited the army to come in and take over. The army has been there ever since.

Sterling's testimony is worthy of note because there is nothing to prevent the Uruguay scenario from being repeated. Even the strongest nations are vulnerable to such techniques. Indeed, the strategy of terror, of killing innocents, or of deploying force against the established order and civility has been used frequently throughout the world over the last dozen years with mixed results--all too often, successful results. The formula is derived from Carlos Marighella's Minimanual of the Urban Guerrilla, which discusses the use of terrorism as a means to force the government into repressive measures.

It is important to note that Americans and American property abroad are now and have been the target of terrorists with increasing frequency. In 1982, according to the CIA, a total of 385 international terrorist incidents were directed against American citizens or property. That was more than any other year since 1968, with the exception of 1978, when hundreds of attacks occurred in Iran. In 1982 we were victimized by six kidnappings, seven assassinations and 160 bombings of U.S. property. Moreover, all of the Americans killed by international terrorist attacks in 1980, 1981, and 1982 were attacked because of their nationality. In previous years, by contrast, most were victims of indiscriminate attack. From 1968 through 1982, 194 Americans were killed in terrorist attacks.

The FBI reports that during 1982 there were 51 terrorist incidents in the United States, including 28 bombings. There is evidence, however, that the actual incidence of domestic terrorism is greater than is reflected in the FBI figures. In testifying to the Subcommittee on Security and Terrorism, the FBI explained that it records a terrorist incident only if credit is claimed by a terrorist group or if the act itself can clearly be ascribed to terrorists.

We should keep in mind, however, that a recitation of past events and numbers does not really even scratch the surface of the breadth and depth of the terrorist problem that could confront us at any time in the United States. Because of the alarming levels which acts of international terrorism had reached and because of the serious implications of terrorism for free societies throughout the world, Senator Thurmond decided in 1980 to form a new Senate Subcommittee on Security and Terrorism. Spreading world terrorism and its implications for our own domestic situation pose too serious a challenge for our government to respond with benign and naive neglect. As elected representatives, we in the Senate had two basic choices about the problem of terrorism. We could wring our hands and shake our heads, or we could use our legislative, fact-finding mandate to try to piece together a picture of what is going on and what has gone on; to make a careful, thorough and dispassionate study to identify the terrorists, their resources, their origin, and their motivations. If we could determine those factors, we might be in a position to make a careful, thoughtful, measured and effective response to future acts of terrorism. Better yet, we might be able to deter future acts of terrorism prior to their occurrence.

The Subcommitttee therefore has the mandate to improve our nation's understanding of and response to terrorism. I believe firmly that as a free people, Americans can and must, to the best of their ability, understand the forces in the world that threaten our way of life. If we understand those forces we can take reasonable and effective steps to help secure for ourselves and for our children a life that is as free as possible from the violence and injustice of terrorism.

As Chairman of the Subcommittee on Security and Terrorism, one of the characteristics of terrorists that has impressed me most is their dependence upon the news media as an indispensable part of their strategy. Each of us is aware that terrorism, by nature, is largely theatrical.

Theatrical productions require a stage, sound amplification, floodlights, publicity, an audience, dissemination, and eager media analysis. The media, by nature, stand ready and--in most cases--willing to provide each of those essential ingredients, thus making a particular terrorist act the audience-riveting spectacle which the perpetrators so desperately desire it to be. Truly, terrorists and the media have a symbiotic relationship, and I do not say that critically. It is just the nature of the media. Were I in it, I am sure that I would be taking the pictures, asking the questions, and so on.

We need to look into the role of the media. We must evaluate to what extent the media has allowed itself to be used and manipulated by terrorists. The truth of the matter is that both law enforcement officials and the American public have become suspicious of the media's treatment of terrorist violence. A Gallup poll taken in April 1977 revealed that the respondents were divided over whether there should continue to be full, detailed coverage of terrorist incidents. Police chiefs in approximately 30 cities were almost unanimous in their belief that live television coverage promotes terrorism. They were unanimously opposed to live transmission. Nearly one-third felt that terrorist incidents should not even be televised at all. Nearly half of the police chiefs said that television coverage poses "a great threat" to the life and limb of hostages and one-third considered television to be "a moderate threat." The attitudes of the great majority of the local law enforcement agents ranged from critical to hostile with respect to the performance of journalists covering terrorist stories. One-third stated that there should be no communication whatsoever between television reporters and terrorists during a terrorist incident, while two-thirds desired that such contact be approved or controlled by law enforcement authorities.

The report of the National Task Force on Disorders and Terrorism, issued more than six years ago, was extremely sensitive to the issue of freedom of the press.

9

Nevertheless, it states "in a relatively small number of situations involving extraordinary violence where emergency condiditions exist or where criminal objectives would be furthered by press coverage, arguments in favor of temporary, limited but effective regulation of the media should be given weight." Instead of government regulation, however, I would much rather that the press--who can't be blamed for ignorance about their effect in supporting the aims of terrorism--be the source of their own self-regulation.

The Hanafi Muslim hostage attack on the B'nai B'rith headquarters in 1977 virtually paralyzed Washington and dramatized the significant problem of the tension between the freedom of the press and government security operations, especially when the latter are directed toward the preservation of human life. It can no longer be said that the media are unaware of their quintessential role in the terror syndrome. In fact, many journalists have become militantly defensive about their coverage of terrorist behavior and they strenuously argue for the public's right to know. The media and their supporters often seek refuge on the higher ground of consitutional principle and democratic philosophy. I am not suggesting that without media reporting, terrorism would cease to exist. Cause and effect are not so vitally linked in this case. I believe, however, that as responsible citizens we must identify what reasonable steps the media could and should take in order to deprive terrorists of the attention they require and the benefits which they derive from that publicity.

Terrorist incidents may not be media-created events but they are undeniably media-promoted events. We can postulate, therefore, that although terrorism is a weapon of the weak, it is self-evident that, deprived of media attention and publicity, terrorism would become a weapon of the impotent. To help bring about that eminently desirable situation, a number of proposals have been formulated:

    1. Prohibit terrorist spokesmen from appearing on camera.

2. Grant news coverage only to those incidents on which reports will serve the public interest.
3. Limit live coverage of terrorist incidents.
4. Omit the names of terrorist groups taking credit for violent incidents.

I realize that defining "public interest" and omitting the names of the terrorist groups are questions which are not simplistically solved. I hope that this gathering today will help lay the foundation for better understanding of how terrorism relies on the media. Once we have that understanding we can develop guidelines by which the media can cover acts of terrorism in a manner that is consistent with our needs both to be informed and to live in a peaceful and secure society.

Charles Fenyvesi
Columnist
The Washington Post

I would like to take you back to 1977. It was a Friday morning at two o'clock when I found myself lying on the concrete floor of an unfinished building in downtown Washington with 107 other hostages. The police came in, our heavily armed captors mysteriously disappeared, huge wire cutters were used to cut off the electric wires that were wound around us, and all of a sudden--it was like a dream--we were allowed to get up. The first thing I did was to look at my watch and establish that it was two o'clock, Friday morning. I said to the fellow who was lying next to me, "I guess I'll make the Sunday paper." The fellow on my left thought that I had a crazy sense of humor. The fellow on my right, who is a very dear friend, said, "Must you write this up?" Later he told me that he felt that the commercialization and the sensationalism that was inherent in the journalistic profession was somehow inconsistent with the kind of coverage of the event that he would have liked to have seen. He thought that serious analysis was all right, but normal, ordinary press coverage was not.

We were escorted to the hotel next door and in ten minutes, in an incredible hustle and bustle, we learned that in those 39 hours that we had been in the building as hostages, the whole world found out about us. There had been interviews on the air and live coverage around the clock. When I talked with the spokesman for the hostages, he said, "Reporters are terrible." Trying to be the spokesman had been a terrible experience for him because he was being squeezed. Later on I learned from a colleague that he had explained his hostility by stating, "I'm anxious about the lives of the people who are in there. You (journalists) only care about your story."

Following our rescue, a police officer and the person who became the prosecuting attorney said to us, "Don't talk to the press. Don't tell them a thing." There was silence.

I was sitting up front and I said, "I'm a reporter." The prosecuting attorney replied, "Well I know your kind, but the best thing you could do is to keep quiet." When the news media representatives finally were able to get through the police cordon, one of them who knew me saw my face and thrust his camera into the bus and asked, "Charlie, how do you feel?" I replied, "I feel wonderful!" You should have heard my fellow hostage colleagues in the back. "Shut up! They're poison! They're not interested in our welfare!" By five o'clock I was home and at seven o'clock there was a knock on my door. It was a good friend of mine from the The Washington Post asking the obvious question. "3,000 words, four o'clock this afternoon. Can you do it?" I gave the obvious answer, "Of course," and I did the story.

In general I felt that the media coverage of the 39 hours was good and fair. I felt that the coverage by The Washington Post, which became my paper two years ago, was good, fair, careful and sensitive. But I also remember three egregious examples of the kind of thing that hostages fear most. In the first six hours, one of the reporters who was standing on the side of the building noticed that a basket was being lowered from the fifth floor of this eight-floor building. By then everyone knew that we were on the eighth floor. The basket, however, was being lowered from the fifth floor and some strange, anxious faces appeared at the window. The reporter immediately jumped to the conclusion that not everyone was on the eighth floor and he also realized that if someone was lowering a basket, then he was hiding from the captors. In other words, he was still a free man, so to speak. The reporter immediately broadcast the incident on the radio. Fortunately, the Hanafi gunmen, their families and their friends, all of whom monitored everything, somehow missed this report. As soon as it happened, listeners called the radio station and the report was not repeated. But this example illustrates that terrorism is a war situation in which a reporter must take sides and must determine whether he is interested in preserving life and helping the hostages, or whether he is interested in getting the scoop.

13

Wayne R. Gilbert
Deputy Assistant Director
Criminal Investigation Division
Federal Bureau of Investigation

Terrorism is one of the top four priorities of the FBI. The other three are organized crime, white collar crime, and foreign-counter intelligence. In 1982, we fortunately had some major successes in combatting terrorism in the United States. Our efforts were most successful in the arena of Armenian and Irish terrorists, where we were able to abort some bombing incidents and to make some significant arrests.

Within the Bureau, the Department of Justice has policy guidelines for relations with the media. They deal specifically with the type of news releases which we are allowed to disseminate in certain types of cases. For example, on fugitive cases we're able to provide much more information than we can on cases pending investigation. Those of you who are in the media have undoubtedly heard spokesmen for the Bureau say repeatedly, "We cannot comment on that case because it's pending investigation." Basically, these guidelines deal with the problem of the public's right to know, balanced with fairness, accuracy, and sensitivity to the rights of the defendants. That's the age-old problem which we face.

Terrorist incidents, by their very nature, are media events. Some people would refer to them as circuses. The Washington Monument takeover is the perfect example. An amateur was making waves. It happened here in Washington on a nice day. The media got so close to the situation that they ran out of things to say. In that case a reporter became actively involved in the negotiation.

Our philosophy which has worked for us in most instances, is that we try to keep the media informed as the event is occurring. We generally designate a specific area and a specific individual so the media can elicit information.

At the same time, we must balance the public's need to know with operational interests such as deployment of personnel, use of diversionary tactics, and certain technical strategies. As Charles Fenyvesi just indicated, the worst case scenario is for some member of the media to broadcast what is going on. I recall the Lake Braddock (Virginia) High School incident several months ago, when a young man had a rifle and was holding twelve hostages. He was in a highly agitated state. A young broadcaster at the local radio station reported that the individual's apparent reason for this incident was that his girlfriend had jilted him. This is the last thing this young man wanted to hear on the radio. That was, as far as he was concerned, a nationwide broadcast that he was inadequate and it came very close to pushing him over the edge and inciting him to kill three or four people. Thus, we must balance these interests in what we make available to the media.

Finally, the bottom line is that we have to prosecute at the conclusion of the incident. Therefore, we have to bear this in mind in deciding what we release to the media. The media representative receives extensive training regarding what he can tell the media. He still, quite frankly, screws up every once in a while. It's a tough position in all of our 59 offices. It's not exactly a sought-after job!

Eugene H. Methvin
Senior Editor
The Reader's Digest

In the year 356 B.C. a fellow named Herostratus, who desired to see his name go down in history and fame amongst all the Greeks, set fire to one of the seven wonders of the ancient world, the beautiful temple of Artemis at Ephesus. His motive was to secure fame. The Greeks reasoned that they would make it a capital punishment to mention the name of Herostratus, but that made it all the more daring and sensational to talk about him. We still hear about Herostratus; his story has gone down in history.

The quest for fame is one of the major quests behind the terrorist action. When the media takes notice of the terrorist and broadcasts both his action and his cause to the whole world, the publicity has a "status-conferral" effect which the terrorist knows and seeks. It is particularly fitting that we are talking about terrorism at the same time the survivors of the Holocaust are meeting in Washington. We often forget that the fellow who started the Holocaust began his career as a terrorist in Munich by seizing hostages. He marched into a beer hall where the ruling state political party was holding a political rally and he, along with his stormtroopers, seized the whole congregation. He marched down the aisle and announced that he was going to take control of the state government and was going to march on Berlin. That night he fumbled a bit: somebody forgot to guard the back door, so his hostages walked out. The next day Hitler led a march on City Hall and several people were killed as the police fired on the march.

That was Hitler's first break into the headlines of the world. Early in his campaign, Hitler learned to overcome the recruiting problem of his party by mixing violence and publicity. He and his stormtroopers would storm into political rallies and create violence. The democratic media, the socialist media, and even the Communist media had to take note of him. That solved the recruiting problem: they were able to build up their party to the point where they could opt for the policy of peaceful politics. In 1936, Hitler's Minister of Radio Propaganda wrote about the way in which the mixture of violence and propaganda creates a lightning effect. "Violence arrests the attention of all who are within sight and hearing of the action...it focuses the attention of everybody in the audience on the terrorists' propaganda message." At that time, Daniel Schorr was a reporter for the Jewish telegraph agency, and years later Schorr wrote that there was a sort of symbiotic relationship between him and the American Nazis that he was covering. They needed publicity and he needed a story. He's had second thoughts about his role in publicizing their activities ever since.

Communists and Marxists around the world have very thoroughly developed the technique of using the media and launching terrorist movements. In Argentina in 1970, the Montoneros, who later expanded to such an extent that they tore up the whole country, were just beginning with five or six members, some of whom had been trained in Cuba. They kidnapped the retired president of the country, Pedro Aramburu, took him out to a farmhouse in the country, held him prisoner, conducted a kangaroo court trial, and then they murdered him. Now, there's no great trick to kidnapping an unarmed, unguarded 67-year-old retired president of a country. It was very easy to do, but this was the Montoneros' way of attracting attention and announcing the existence of their organization. It was a recruiting poster for them. Thus the media has a very strong role in the development of terrorist movements.

In Carlos Marighella's handbook, The Minimanual of the Urban Guerrilla, the author points out, the terrorist units do not even have to be in touch with one another. They can communicate through the media. The important thing is to carry out what he calls "action models" and to raise the level of criminal, terrorist activity within society.

Given that the media has a very important integral role in the propagation of terrorist ideas and recruitment, how can we respond? I would propose that the southern journalists' response to the Ku Klux Klan in the 30's, 40's, and 50's serve as a model. The response was a departure from the dominant tradition of American journalism, i.e., the Hearst and Pulitzer tradition that violence and freaks are news. The southern journalists had a different attitude about it and, as a result, the treatment of terrorist activity in the media in those days was extremely different in the South. Generally speaking, the southern journalists--or at least the better ones--believed that it was their role to attack and ridicule the Klan. Thus there was no semblance of balance or objective coverage in the news columns when it can to dealing with the Klan and others of that ilk.

Finally, I'd like to quote Steve Rosenfeld of The Washington Post who said "If the purpose of terrorists is to send a message, we of the media should consider not sending it."

The Honorable Frank H. Perez
Deputy Director
Office for Combatting Terrorism
U.S. Department of State

Since I spent the last three and a half years working on international terrorism, I would like to examine U.S. press coverage of international terrorism. I think that the statements made earlier about the press being used by the terrorists are absolutely correct. The press is very important to the terrorist in terms of getting their message out, engendering sympathy and support for their cause, articulating their demands, and putting pressure on both governments and populations.

The United States press seems to be mostly event-oriented. Every terrorist event which occurs is reported. You may find it reported in two or three lines on the last page of a newspaper. It is very shallow reporting, lacking any real analysis. Thus the American public is not gaining an appreciation for terrorist events and what they mean. Today, for example, an American Shell Oil executive who had been taken hostage in Bogota was released. I don't expect to see any analytical reporting on what it all meant. But if you look at Colombia, there have been over 80 kidnappings of well-to-do citizens and executives since the first of the year. These events are having a very severe impact on the business community there. There ought to be more balanced analysis rather than mere superficial reporting of these events.

Clearly the press is being used by terrorists who are advancing their objectives. I believe in freedom of the press, but I think it can be more responsible in the way it deals with the issues it covers. For example, the Maze Prison hunger strike was covered extensively. During the summer when things were dull in the news, there was a great deal of reporting about the striking IRA prisoners. In effect, the reports created sympathy for the terrorists, despite the violent acts they had committed and the many innocent people they had killed or injured. The coverage generated a lot of sympathy in this country, and as a consequence, it generated considerable funds which have gone into the terrorists' coffers for more weapons to kill more people.

The Armenian terrorists have now killed some 26 Turkish diplomats. Articles reporting on these killings always discuss the so-called Armenian genocide as a rationale for the violence. I have never seen any real analysis of the significance of all of this and the effect that it's having around the world. Clearly what the Armenians are doing is emulating the Palestinians who they feel have made great gains in public recognition through these acts of terrorism. I don't think the press has really picked up on this or adequately reported on it. The coverage of the Teheran hostage situation was another terrible mistake. We gave too much prominence and too much attention to that situation. We thus increased the leverage of Khomeini over the United States government and over the people.

Reporting on terrorism requires better judgment to focus on what the real issues are. Restraint, coupled with a clearer perspective, is needed.

Ford Rowan, Esq.
Host
"International Edition" (PBS)

Discussing media coverage of terrorist incidents reminds me of what Gibbon wrote on another subject: "It is easier to deplore than to describe." I will try to describe it anyway. Terrorism is an act of theater and, unfortunately, the media is its stage. The press, and especially the electronic media, seems to thrive on the sensational. The terrorists, for their part, manufacture sensations to capture the attention of the fascinated public.

Bill Green, once the ombudsman of The Washington Post questioned the role of the media in the Iranian hostage crisis and asked, "Was the press in any degree a party to the Iranian attack? Should it have been more cautious? Did it lose its cool? Did the press, by writing and broadcasting feverish bits of news, inflame the situation? If so, did it have alternatives?" I think those questions look at the problem from the point of view of how the press operates. Questions about the appropriate limit of news coverage, or the necessity of self-censorship do not evidence an understanding of the way news judgments are made.

First of all, what is news? A network anchorman once defined news as "News is what I say it is." Aside from the inherent arrogance in that statement, it is true. News is what the newspeople say it is. I don't know a better definition. When you turn on your television every night and want to know what the news is, it is what you see in the newscast. This means that there is a lot of peer group pressure regarding what is covered. If ABC is covering a hostage crisis night after night, you can be quite sure that the other networks are not going to ignore it. That's a safety device for society. Competition insures that there will be a free flow of information.

On the other hand, occasionally there is pack journalism where reporters follow the leader--or follow the

21

scramble. (I don't think there is a leader.) The press is interested in the unusual, the dramatic, the sensational, the surprising, the violent. And terrorist incidents fall perfectly into this category. News coverage is event-oriented; it is not issue-oriented. The press is dependent upon its sources, and its sources--ranging from the President of the United States, who always has media access, to the guy who seizes the local police chief in Cleveland at the end of a gun--are self-interested. Reporters may not like to be dependent and may try to avoid being too co-opted by their sources, but it is a fact of life that journalism, as it has developed in this country, requires sources.

Reporters are not regarded as independent fountains of knowledge; they report what others do and say. Walter Laqueur said that media access is a selective magnifying glass, enormously attracted to terrorism because of its mystery, quick action, tension and drama. The terrorists in turn depend on that publicity and attention. Virgil Dominick, the news director of a Cleveland television station, admitted after one terrorist incident: "The coverage is partly to blame, for we are glorifying law-breakers. In effect, we are losing control over our news department. We are being used." On the other hand, to ignore such incidents would be a risk, creating a credibility gap on the part of the public's belief in what they see on television.

Press coverage is competitive. That is good and bad. The good part is that it is unlikely that major facts will be kept from the American public. The press does not join conspiracies to withhold information. Democracy works best that knows most. On the other hand, competitive pressures can get out of hand. The Iranian hostage crisis, again, is a case in point. All three networks were offered the chance to get the first exclusive interview with an American hostage. Two of them turned it down (rightly, I think) because of the terrorists' conditions: there had to be a live, unedited platform for a statement by a terrorist spokesman. Reflection and calm determination of what's going on is essential in these cases. Unfortunately, however, most of the coverage is live, and because there is no editing, live coverage is most prone to mistakes or inadvertant, inflammatory statements.

The question of whether the press should censor itself asks the wrong question. We should look at it from the other point of view. What is newsworthy? What should the press select from the umpteen trillion things that happen today? Which are the most important? If you decide that a hostage incident cannot be overlooked, then the question is in which context it should be placed. To suppress information entirely risks undermining the credibility not only of the press but of the public officials who would be commenting on these incidents. Suppression increases the likelihood of rumor, leading, in the worst of all cases, to even more violent behavior by the publicity seekers.

Self-restraint is really the only answer. The CBS standards on this topic are excellent. The guidelines state that there are no specific self-executing rules. The normal tests of news judgment must apply. These tests, however, are sometimes left aside in the mad scramble to get information, to get it first, and to get it on line. If a story is newsworthy under the CBS standards, it should be covered, despite the dangers of contagion.

The CBS standards note that suppression of information would be counter-productive. They call for conscientious care and restraint. Specifically, demands of terrorists should be reported, but putting the terrorists themselves on the air should be avoided. Except in rare cases, there should not be live coverage, providing the unedited platform. News reporters should be careful in using phone calls to the terrorists. Phone lines should not be used if they will interfere with the authorities' efforts to get through to the terrorists. Experts should be contacted to see what terminology should be avoided and for guidance in not making things worse; guidance--not control. The standards call for cooperation with local authorities in gathering information and avoiding inflammatory statements or pat words. The coverage of such incidents should not unduly crowd out coverage of other important news.

The CBS guidelines are worthy of reflection. They are an indication of the kind of imperfect but necessary solution to the problems of over-coverage and over-inflammatory news interest in terrorist activities.

George Watson
Vice President
ABC News

Yesterday and this morning I was in Jacksonville, Alabama with a group of people concerned about the recent tragedy there that attracted so much media attention when a man tried to burn himself. The incident raised the question of the responsibility of journalists who are confronted with situations in which their actions might save a life or prevent an injury--or, alternatively, might cause those tragedies to occur. One person expressed a great deal of skepticism about self-censorship of certain news because it supposedly does not comport with the processes or institutions of society. He recalled incidents in Thelma, Alabama in 1960 when people protesting the rigidly segregated society in Alabama were regarded as terrorists of a sort--people who had forsaken law and order, were intent on disturbing the peace, and were--in the views of many, if not most of the citizens of Alabama--quite beyond the pale of civil or civilized behavior.

These comments make me very skeptical of many of the ideas I've heard this afternoon, i.e. that we should not tell people what is going on inside the Maze prison or that we are providing a platform for terrorists. Yes, we are, in a sense, providing a platform. And, as Mr. Perez suggests, we do need more understanding and analysis. If we had understood and acted on our understanding of the grievances of the Palestinian people, it is possible that they might not have reverted to the acts of outragious terrorism which they have perpetrated. It is not, however, the responsibility of the media to decide that this lot is good or bad and that we ought not provide a platform for their grievances when they involve terrorist actions. Our basic responsibility is to report what is happening. Senator Denton has said that we have a symbiotic relationship with terrorists. That is true, but we also have a symbiotic relationship with Senator Denton and his colleagues, with law enforcement officials, and with everyone else about whom we report.

When Mr. Gilbert mentioned the role of an Associated Press reporter in the seizure of the Washington monument, he neglected to mention that the reporter was drafted by the law enforcement officials to perform that role. A similar scenario occurred at Sing Sing late last year when the Governor of New York and his representatives asked ABC News to allow our correspondent to go into the prison. We were very precise in specifying that we did not regard that as his role, but the prisoners who were holding the guards hostage wanted a representative of the press, and the law enforcement officials decided that that suited their strategy. We <u>reluctantly</u> agreed. So very often in the coverage of terrorists and hostage episodes we find ourselves in an uneasy alliance with law enforcement officials because we are obviously and understandably and, I hope, intelligently concerned about not making a bad situation worse.

The Hanafi Moslem incident which Charles Fenyvesi recalled was a landmark event in "raising the consciousness" of journalists and law enforcement officials with regard to covering and dealing with terrorist episodes. That was also the event which led to the drafting of guidelines for CBS, ABC and many other news organizations. If the guidelines were laid out in their entirety and if we sat down with the representatives from the FBI and various police departments (particularly those in the larger cities with officers who specialize in handling hostage incidents and terrorist episodes), we would find ourselves in general agreement about our respective roles and responsibilities. It seems to me that the guidelines have worked fairly well.

I think Ford Rowan errs in stating that most of the coverage of terrorist episodes is live. Most of it, in fact, is taped and edited. I agree that live coverage is a serious problem. The guidelines have strictures against it except in "the most compelling circumstances," whatever they may be. The definition of "most compelling" obviously invites differences of opinion. As Wayne Gilbert said, we are certainly capable of screwing up. We have done it in the past, and we will almost certainly do it in the future.

My final point is that the popular way of addressing this problem is to round up some of the usual suspects, as we have done this afternoon, to talk for an hour or so. Useful as that is, there is something lacking. The media and the law enforcement officials need to develop better ways to understand how we act and react in situations of this sort. Yonah Alexander has suggested the development of sophisticated simulations to inform both journalists and law enforcement officials of the complexities of the problem and the ways to deal with these complexities. Let's do it! ABC News enlisted the cooperation of Georgetown University's Center for Strategic and International Studies in producing a television program that gave the audience a better understanding of the dynamics of a terrorist episode and how those with responsibility might deal with it. Tough, challenging simulations that really force the participants to think about past and potential terrorist situations could be useful. By all means, let's talk about the issues, but let's also devise some new means of testing our actions, our reactions, and their potential consequences.

QUESTIONS FROM THE AUDIENCE

Aaron Rosenbaum
Rosenbaum Associates, Washington, DC

I agree with the statements made by George Watson and Ford Rowan that the media generally report things reasonably fully and accurately, but I'd like to pose a question on a deeper level, dealing with cultural considerations as Westerners and with subcultural considerations as journalists. First, with respect to the issue of ignorance and superficiality on the part of the reporters: obviously they can't be experts on everything and they can't get an in-depth education all at once, especially as something new breaks. The question is one of willful ignorance, of knowing that something is a staged performance (for example, the reports of staged Christmases for the POW's in Vietnam). My second point concerns the issue of preconceptions about the nature of grievances, romanticizing the terrorist and implying that the terrorist is, by definition, naturally aggrieved. Finally, the assumption that is really cultural is that terrorists are operating on our level of civilization and are interested in dialectic. Can you address these problems of culture and subculture?

Ford Rowan

First of all, you are right in stating that reporters cannot be experts about everything, and most generally-assigned reporters (constituting the majority of reporters) are not experts on anything. Too often, it is flying by the seat of your pants; you just do the best you can.

I don't like the term "willful ignorance." Yes, there are a lot of staged performances. Senator Denton's hearings are in effect staged performances, aren't they? Terrorist incidents are geared for press coverage, and therefore the reporter must say that it's a staged incident. That should be made clear in their reporting. In most of the coverage of terrorist events, reporters do make it clear that the terrorists want publicity.

As for preconceptions, there is some romanticizing-but not much. Reporters keep their eye on the dangers involved. It is difficult to glorify or glamorize what someone's doing to an innocent victim. In many cases the assumption that the terrorists are like us, wanting only to talk and be heard, is a false assumption. But the opposite can also be portrayed: that the terrorists are a bunch of fanatics and madmen from the seventh century and there's no way to talk to them at all.

The question about the press's perception of what is happening is a very difficult one because we all carry around attitudes and mindsets which have been ingrained in us over the years. This creates what is called "bias" in the press. But it is not the kind of partisan bias so often alleged. It is a middle-class bias. Most of the press is middle-class and most of the press looks at the world that way; it's hard not to. For any of us who have ever tried to put ourselves in the other person's shoes, it's not an easy thing to do, and sometimes it's painful.

Eugene Methvin

George Watson talked earlier about reporting the causes of terrorism. That presumes that you have to look at the grievances of the terrorists as well. For example, what were Hitler's grievances when he seized the hostages in the beer hall? What were Stalin's grievances? The fact is that a lot of these people want power, they want fame, and they want to realize and act out their messianic beliefs. If we're going to get into the causes and grievances and so on, we have to analyze the psychology of the terrorists.

George Watson

However criminal terrorists in a given incident may have been, whatever outrageous motives may have caused them to act, I would not have wished for the news accounts to be suppressed. I'd want to know about it, and I'd want to know about the reasons why they did it. The terrorists of one generation often become the country's leaders of another generation. Therefore, I don't think the newsmen should make the judgment that a group is beyond the pale. They may have very legitimate grievances, and it may behoove us to know what they are.

Finally, I agree with Ford Rowan's statement that NBC made a wrong call when they agreed to broadcast a statement by "Typhoid Mary," the Iranian hostage, in exchange for an interview with Marine William Gallegos. My overall impression, however, is that Typhoid Mary failed to win any converts for the Ayatollah among the people who saw that interview. Quite the contrary: the reaction of most of those who saw the broadcast was that our citizens were in the hands of some crazy people.

Edmond Jacoby
The Washington Times

I hear people saying that reporters are inadequately trained. They do tend to be a rough bunch; they are not good at walking on eggs. Would you suggest that we need people to be trained specifically to examine and report on terrorist events? Does ABC have people who are specifically selected to deal with reporting terrorist activities for the network?

George Watson

No, we don't have people who are experts in covering terrorism. We certainly have people with gray hair, or with no hair, who have covered many terrorist incidents and who bring to us, I hope, an accumulation of wisdom and expertise on how to deal with such incidents. It is true, however, that more likely than not when a terrorist episode erupts, the reporters covering it are relatively inexperienced in that field. I don't know if it is reasonable to imagine a cadre of experts who would be sent out like a SWAT team to cover terrorist episodes whenever and wherever they occurred. Certainly there are people who are recognized experts. We use Claire Sterling quite frequently on "Nightline." We may call in a variety of experts when a terrorist incident occurs, but we do not have reporters who are assigned to cover terrorism as they are assigned to cover the White House.

Eugene Methvin

I would think that any major daily that has an expert on batting averages or the local professional ball club ought to have an expert adept at covering political extremists.

George Watson

We don't have an expert on batting averages, either!

Martin Arostegui
Risks Institute, Alexandria, Virginia

Since the media is responsible for covering events in an informal manner, perhaps they should be responsible for creating a cadre of experts--a SWAT team--to cover terrorist events. If they don't, they're not being functional.

George Watson

I don't disagree that all of our reporters should understand and be instructed in the ABC guidelines and policies dealing with covering a terrorist episode. But I don't think it is reasonable to imagine that you could have a terrorist correspondent that you pop off to Memphis, Tennessee one day, the Washington Monument another day, and so on. The business of journalism doesn't work that way. The New York Times doesn't have such a correspondent, none of the wire services do, and I am not entirely sure that the volume of the terrorist episodes actually requires it.

Charles Fenyvesi

I believe that the volume of expertise on the subject of terrorism and particularly on the subject of the news media's responsibility in covering terrorism is not that great. But if you were to be sent out as a special correspondent to Northern Ireland, to Israel, or to some yet-to-be-named location of terrorist violence, I think one hour would be enough to establish procedural guidelines. What you need is a bit of common sense, which is something that most reporters have, and a sense of history, which is something that many reporters do lack. But I don't think you need a Ph.D. in Terrorology. You need some extra sensitivity and a list of things to avoid.

One other observation: as much as I am grateful to the police--federal and local--for what they did in our instance and in other instances, I am very happy that some of my colleagues--invited or not--participated in the negotiations with the terrorists.

Joel Lisker, Esq.
Chief Counsel
Subcommittee on Security and Terrorism (Judiciary)
U.S. Senate

I was struck and even shocked by some of Mr. Watson's comments. I recognize that perhaps we come from different ends of the spectrum. However, if a media figure interjects himself into a terrorist situation, then he has a responsibility beyond merely having a high school education and an interest in collecting news. If he's going to place the lives of innocent people in possible jeopardy on the strength of some ethereal reason like the public's right to know (whatever that means), then he has responsibilities. I don't see how he can simply side-step this responsibility, and say, "Well, I'm just here to get the facts, to get the story." If a terrorist group raids an orphanage, I could care less about why they chose to do so. It is an act of terror, no matter what. I see no reason for the media to become a surrogate for the terrorist, attempting to explain in some rational way why this poor guy is killing these children.

George Watson

But you do want to know that the orphanage has been attacked, do you not?

Joel Lisker

If that means that additional lives may be in danger, I am not sure that I do want to know.

George Watson

You are interjecting another concern which I share. I don't want to do anything that jeopardizes lives. Among our guidelines are the clear instructions that we obey all the instructions given by the police and that we seek their guidance in how a situation can be covered without loss of life. It is certainly not our role to interject ourselves into such situations. I am strenuously opposed to our seeking any mediating role or even an inside role. I am not entirely happy with saying "Just let the police handle it," because they are capable of mishandling things as well. But I don't think it is our role to interject ourselves into the situation.

Morris Leibman

In concluding this panel discussion, I would like to add one final point regarding the intellectual debate about Western civilization versus tyrannies. When we worry about the potential for war, I would give nuclear war a negative one on a scale of ten; conventional war a one; and naval engagements a one and a half. The real terrain in the next ten years will be psychological war, guerrilla warfare, assassinations, and terrorism. This whole field will require the participation and skills of all the social scientists including lawyers, academics, journalists, and broadcasters. It is a new world and a new terrain. We ought to understand that the enemy has accepted terrorism as a specialized profession to which they have devoted a great deal of training, monetary investment, and research. It is up to us to catch up.

Leonard J. Theberge and John McLaughlin

Ford Rowan

The Honorable Diego C. Asencio and Dean Robert Morrissey, SUNY

George Watson and Yonah Alexander

Morris I. Leibman

Eugene H. Methvin

Leonard J. Theberge, Morris I. Leibman, Yonah Alexander and Wayne R. Gilbert

Panel Two: Overseas Experience

Moderator: Dr. John McLaughlin
"The McLaughlin Group" (NBC)
Moderator

    I have the impression, which you must have developed already for yourselves, that there is a curious symbiotic relationship between journalists and terrorists. It is sometimes a diseased relationship in that the political act itself, or the symbolic terrorist act, has no real meaning or value without the attendant publicity. Terrorism flourishes on publicity and on the manipulation of mass media by the terrorist. It is a rudimentary and necessary ingredient in his strategy. It has been said that journalists are the terrorists' best friends. Let us then begin our exploration through the lens of international or overseas experience of this peculiar situation existing in the world today.

The Honorable Diego C. Asencio
Assistant Secretary for Consular Affairs
U.S. Department of State

I assume that I am on the panel to present a viewpoint from the perspective of the victim. In 1980, as Ambassador to Colombia, I happened to be attending National Day celebrations at the Dominican Embassy. Some people came in and started shooting at the ceiling. We wound up in a barricade situation, with an extensive shoot-out lasting several hours.

One of the first things that struck me during my captivity, which was to last 61 days, was that a group of hostages became part of the negotiation process, thus departing from the usual developments in a hostage situation. We decided that if we were going to get out of there in one piece, we would have to take an active role in setting up discussion between the Colombian government and the terrorists. Such a dialogue could not be considered a given because the Colombian government had stated clearly that it does not deal with terrorists on a discussion or negotiation basis.

Our first discovery was that the telephone lines were clogged by journalists, preventing us from calling out to try to establish the links that were necessary to set up the discussions. It took the better part of three days to work out the ground rules for a government-terrorist negotiating conference. Those three days we thus dealt with an additional cross to bear as we had to keep telling people to get off the phone. In a substantial number of cases, they would refuse, which meant that we could not call out. This was something that, at that particular juncture when things were a bit tense, did not endear them to us.

The other aspect which struck me was that as journalists attempted to get close to the action, the terrorists habitually put me on the windowsill and shot at them from the vicinity of my right kneecap--a habit which contributed a bit to the pucker factor, and which was a fairly interesting but undesirable arrangement from my standpoint! It also did not sit well with the group of hostages, and it was the beginning of a very, very tense approach to our predicament on our part. In effect, a sort of tent city of journalists grew up in front of the Dominican Mission. The Mission was in the middle, surrounded by a barricade of security forces, and the tent city was in the distance, waiting, presumably, to report our demise. In fact, they reported my demise at least twice, with all the attendant impact that had on my family back in the United States, the American Embassy, and so on.

Terrorism is the original cheap shot and is not really cost effective even as a cheap shot unless there is publicity. For instance, in our particular case, the terrorists were asking for the return of 311 political prisoners and $50 million. They did not get their political prisoners and they got precious little money. But they did get a heck of a play not only in the Colombian press but in the world press as well.

Looking at the issue of terrorism from the standpoint of a Foreign Service Officer who has been abroad, I am concerned by the possibility that we could be at the beginning of some sort of terrorism cycle. The United States has been enormously lucky, but it is possible that politics in a different guise will be transported here. At some point, if legislators are prevailed upon, they might pass restrictive legislation addressed to the treatment of this particular area. My problem is that I am quite content with the Bill of Rights as it is currently practiced. I would prefer that the media, and particularly television, establish good guidelines to avoid a situation where terrorists and the media are feeding on each other.

Dr. W. Scott Thompson
Associate Director for Programs
U.S. Information Agency

My comments will touch upon four different areas: 1) the philosophical nature of terrorism; 2) the responsibility of the media with respect to terrorism; 3) the Soviet connection; and 4) U.S. nuclear arms security.

My philosophical approach is based on the old question of whether anyone has the right to cry "fire" in a crowded theater. We are dealing with an inflamed issue at a time of rapid technological advance. If the people are the source of rights in a society, then rights have to be exercised contingent upon the benefits to the society. The operation of government and the media alike involve responsibilities to the society that may, at a time of threat, restrain the exercise of our rights. During perilous times in the past, we always have accepted some constraints. Given the unprecedented character of the threat that may be coming upon us, however, we might have to start considering the possibility of being able to accept constraints at short notice. I am not proposing constraints on freedom of the press. I am asking us to learn to anticipate critical situations where such steps might have to be taken. We all know that if there were a dramatic and sudden nuclear threat, there wouldn't be any question that society would accept whatever constraints were necessary to save the millions of lives that were at stake. Let's see if we can have preemptive deterrence on this issue so that we never have to get to that point. One hopes that this kind of constraint can be developed by the international media rather than unilaterally imposed by government.

With respect to the media, the technology that creates our interdependent world--the global village--is obviously the same technology that creates special vulnerabilities and unprecedented power. An Office of Technology Assessment (O.T.A.) study noted that modern air travel and mass communications provide terrorists with mobility and an audience. The vulnerabilities are proceeding much faster than increased interdependence of a positive character. The technology that produces over half a trillion kilowatt hours of nuclear power in the United States obviously enables a terrorist group to make a really super-human threat. I heard an expert on our defense systems point out that prior to the Reagan Administration's security measures, three fellows with wire cutters could have disabled the entire American deterrent capability if they knew exactly what to do. Luckily, no one had that knowledge, or if anyone did, no one tried to exercise it.

The O.T.A. study also states that little can be done to prevent such threats except to minimize the expectations that they will result in organizational gains or personal gratification. For that purpose, the report continues, the less discussion of threats the better. Since the activities of criminals, psychopaths and pranksters often establish a fashion or pattern that is repeatedly emulated, governments at all levels should attempt to conceal the existence of such threats or activities unless there is good reason to believe that the threat is real.

It has been said that the media are the star actors in the terrorist play. The media can incite terror in certain circumstances. But if the media were not to cover terrorist events, terrorists might accelerate the level of violence in order to attract public attention. Any attempt by a democratic government to dictate unilaterally a code of ethics would be a serious mistake. Such ethics must emerge from within, and, I hope, from discussions like this. Terrorism is a form of communication and all countries are vulnerable to it.

With respect to the Soviet connection, it is clear that the KGB is engineering international terrorism. The facts can be proven: they are documented and are well known to the international Western intelligence community. We are not talking about comic book concepts of international plots where the KGB masterminds every little thing. Rather, they work by proxy, letting forces loose, letting forces be interconnected, and playing upon our own weaknesses. In other words, in a modest sort of way, there is already a state of war in existence to which we must respond with certain constraints if we are going to protect ourselves. Again, I am not proposing specific constraints by democratic societies. I am hoping that the press will begin to study this issue very carefully to determine the signals which should activate certain levels of self-constraint in time of emergency.

Finally, in terms of U.S. nuclear weapons security overseas, there has been considerable improvement. But the research and development which goes forward also allows new vulnerabilities and opportunities to which we always have to be sensitive. The potential threat from radical groups has been one of the many concerns we have considered jointly with our allies, and we continue to act in concert with the appropriate nations to ensure that all measures possible are taken to guarantee the future physical integrity of our storage sites overseas. While the safety of these sites has improved, it is not something about which we can relax our guard nor which we can take lightly.

Nicholas Ashford
Washington Bureau Chief
The Times (London)

Having looked at the questions which Yonah Alexander has put before us, it would seem that the main aim of this seminar is to examine whether some form of control of the media is both practical and desirable as a means of combatting or at least limiting the impact of the scourge of terrorism. But before we consider what we in the media can or should do, it is important to reflect briefly on the political nature of terrorism and the organizations that perpetrate terrorist incidents.

Most acts of terrorism are carried out for political reasons. Even the Baader-Meinhof gang in Germany and the Red Brigades in Italy have a political basis for their actions, however distorted they may appear to most of us. In some cases, terrorist organizations are striving to achieve political objectives that many decent men and women would regard as reasonable. It is the means rather than the aims which are to be deplored.

There are a number of incidents in recent history when the terrorist of yesterday emerges as the respected political leader of today. For example, Menachem Begin was once a terrorist whose organization, the Ergun, used murder and bombings to support their objective of establishing a Jewish state in Palestine. The publicity which those activities received in the media, particularly here in the United States, contributed to the pressure placed on Britain to establish an independent state of Israel. The PLO uses the same sort of weapon today to regain what they regard as the Palestinian homeland.

The closing pages of Britain's imperial history are littered with other examples of terrorists who have become statesmen. The late President Kenyatta who once headed a particularly obnoxious organization, the Mau-Mau, emerged as the head of the most stable, pro-Western state in Africa.

In southern Africa, Robert Mugabe and Joseph Nkomo used error as part of their strategy for independence for Zimbabwe. Yet Mugabe was internationally acclaimed when he attempted to set up a government of national unity after independence. Ian Smith, who constantly denounced Mugabe as a terrorist in the past, now sits in the parliamentary chamber with him. In Britain, there is general condemnation of the barbarous methods used by the IRA, and there is very little sympathy for the organization's political aim for a united Ireland. Yet, internationally, and particularly in the United States, there is much greater support for the IRA's political objectives, if not the methods which it used to achieve them. It may well be that if a united Ireland is ever achieved, the gunmen who are now killing and maiming will be acclaimed as heroes and be elevated to political posts.

The purpose of this rather lengthy preamble is to point out that terrorism is at least as much a political problem as it is a security problem. Therefore, any attempts to curb media coverage of terrorist activities must be seen as a form of political censorship. Any democracy handles the weapon of censorship with a great deal of caution, for when it *is* used, it can often prove to be counter-productive. One must acknowledge, however, that one of the most important weapons in the terrorist arsenal is publicity. A terrorist needs the media just as much as a film star does. The whole point of a terrorist action is for it to impact as many people as possible. The murder of an insignificant official in the back streets of Beirut would barely receive mention in the press today. But the gunning down of an internationally known figure, such as Dr. Isam Satawe at an international conference in Portugal is guaranteed to make headline news. The message contained by his murder was quickly grasped by King Hussein.

In Britain, the IRA has skillfully exploited the propaganda value of terrorism. When things start getting tough for them in Northern Ireland, they turn to soft targets in England: a bomb in the car of a Member of Parliament; a bomb in the foyer of the Hilton Hotel; a bomb which decimated a troop of horse carts on their way to a ceremonial parade. Such events are certain to redirect the international spotlight on the IRA, particularly here in the United States. American interest in the Irish problem has grown enormously since the IRA began its present campaign of violence over a decade ago. Funds donated by American sympathizers have grown as well. By calling itself an army, the IRA has skillfully conveyed the impression among many Irish Americans that it is a bona fide force fighting a British army of occupation rather than a group of fanatics who are not representative of the overall majority of the Irish people.

The propaganda effect of terrorism, however, is a two-edged sword. While acts of terror attract public attention, they also provoke public condemnation and revulsion. There seems little doubt, for example, that the murder of Lord Mountbatten was counter-productive in propaganda terms, particularly here in the U.S. This, in a sense, is the main argument against trying to control news about terrorist acts. People who kill and maim should be seen for what they are: fanatics who, however exalted their political aims may be, are essentially thugs and gangsters.

Can or should media coverage of terrorist activities be controlled? I don't think so, largely for the reasons I have just given. Curbs on press coverage not only would deprive the public of its right to know, they also would be almost impossible to enforce. How, for instance, can you keep a murder or a bombing quiet for long? The only sort of control which I favor would be on the flow of information while a terrorist action, such as hijacking or a siege, is underway. Clearly, it is in no one's interest if the terrorists are given any inkling as to the authorities' strategy for dealing with the situation. For instance, the SAS release of the hostages taken at the Iranian Embassy in London three years ago could have been a disaster if the captors had learned of the rescue mission on TV, which was covering the event live. Withholding information from the press in such circumstances is entirely justified.

But beyond that, I fear that international terrorism is a phenomenon of the late twentieth century, facilitated as much by the ease of international travel as by the media. We must hope that the security authorities will succeed in controlling it as much as possible. As for the press, it is our duty to report such events as accurately, objectively and--most importantly--as unsensationally as possible. It is important to understand the political motives that trigger acts of terrorism, and--where possible--to determine whether they can be remedied. At the same time, the public should know how cruel and vicious people can be in pursuit of these objectives.

Ali Birand
Washington Correspondent
Milliyet (Turkey)

I am not a terrorist expert, but I would like to discuss the attitude of the Western press towards terrorism from the perspective of a Turkish journalist. And believe me, it's not very easy to be Turkish nowadays. We work in a very harsh, hostile environment. But I must say that I am proud to be a Turk, and I do not find anything to be ashamed about. Therefore, I am going to talk about Armenian terrorism.

The press has been accused of making statements which indirectly encourage the murder of innocent people, especially in the Armenian case. Armenian terrorism is the unique example of cooperation between the press and a terrorist organization. The Armenian terrorists use publicity more than any other group, even the PLO. The Armenian problem has been in existence since 1973, and suddenly someone has decided that this problem should come to the fore; people should be killed to get the public's attention and Turks should be punished.

In all of these developments, the press has played a very important role. I will give you a concrete scenario that we frequently see in Europe. In some of the capitals which are not friendly to Turkey, leading Armenians give interviews. A very important one was the interview with Armenian leaders in Athens, announcing that a high-level diplomat was going to be killed. Four days later, a diplomat was killed in Belgrade. Capitals are selected to maximize the impact. The identity of the person hit is also very important. Another interesting element of Armenian terrorism is that the Armenians do not kill every day. They give a break to propaganda machines, and then when they see it is dying down, they attack again.

News that a Turkish Ambassador has been killed is generally coupled with commentary on how the Armenians were murdered by those Turks seventy years ago. Suddenly the murderers become freedom fighters. You don't really see the Turkish view in these programs. Even the moderate views are not communicated. There are quite a number of Armenians who say they understand the motives of these terrorists, but they are against their activities themselves.

What is interesting is the double standard of the Western media. It supports the Armenian terrorist, but the PLO terrorist is ugly. Armenian terrorists have gone beyond simple retribution for past events. First of all, the moderate Armenians are increasingly identified with the terrorists. As the Turks see that in every country there is a Turkish diplomat killed, they will be less inclined to recognize the Armenians--even the moderate ones.

Marino de Medici
U.S. Correspondent
Il Tempo (Rome)

The Roman press has been the center of wide controversy and elicits a lot of breast beating and discussion. Asking us to judge our performance in very, very difficult years of Italian history is like asking us to take X-rays of ourselves, knowing that some of the radiation may be very harmful.

There is no doubt that the events in Italy during the 70's were cataclysmic in many ways. Italy is a very complex country. The easy explanation is almost never the right explanation. Let me preface my comments, however, by saying that the press will play a major role when this period of Italy's history is written fifty years from now. It will be a history of how Italy became the seventh--and possibly the sixth--industrial power in the Western world, how our society changed so dramatically and so rapidly, and how our political order was buffeted and misunderstood. The press has had a part not only in terms of recording history but also as a responsible participant that could have done much better than it did. That is not an apology or a confession but simply an objective statement.

In Italy, the press has not been a carrier of news or even a forum for debate. It has been a political propagandist, effectively employed by political parties. It is a very free press, mind you; it is extremely free. I challenge anyone to produce a press which is freer than the press in Italy. But it has played, consciously or unconsciously, into the hands of political forces.

Terrorism has been the litmus test of the attitudes and the behavior of the Italian press throughout these tragic and dramatic years. The press in Italy, after all, mirrors the strength and blemishes of a society that has changed markedly during a time of terrorism. There is no doubt, for instance, that reporting on terrorism in Italy was viewed in large part as acquiesence with the Communists. There was, in fact, something more than toleration for extremes when the Communist Party derived benefits from the more vigorous forms of challenges to the established order, i.e. terrorism.

Let's not forget how the Red Brigades were formed. They had their roots in the university. As long as the challenge was limited to the university, many people in Italy felt that there was nothing wrong. The Communist-controlled press and the left wing press had sharp orders, but they were the kind you give to children when they exceed the rules of the game. But then they became really vicious. The Red Brigades started to shoot--not only police officers and officials, but journalists as well. Things got worse. Still, there was initial sympathy for the action of the Red Brigades--sympathy that was encouraged by the press.

We had a spirited debate regarding what the press should do to combat terrorism, to keep the terrorists from reaching the front pages of the newspapers. Because they did use the newspapers, radio and television very effectively and cleverly. The press was almost reduced to a mailman; in fact some journalists were almost proud that they were the carriers of news for the Red Brigades. It became a mad situation because often when the terrorists called newspapermen to tell them where a communique had been hidden, the police were wiretapping the newspaper. So there was a race to the mailbox to see who would get there first, the policemen or the journalist. We may smile about this now, but when a picture of a judge on the front page of the magazine L'Expresso appeared with the entire transcript of his "interrogation" by the Red Brigades, people finally began to ask the right questions. What usefulness did this have? What did this have to do with the public's right to know? The article was a long, rambling interrogation of a judge whose haggard face expressed his torment at being submitted to this inhumane treatment.

People's hearts began to change and the tide began to

turn in Italy. Change came because of the firm determination by the authorities to crack down on terrorism and because of the improved police force coordination and efficiency. But the most important factor leading to change was popular resolve. People were sick and tired. Italy stood the test of terrorism. The Red Brigades did not manage to convince the Italians that they should be the catalyst for changing the system. It is interesting that a new maturity came about in the country because of this dramatic experience.

Shalom Kital
Washington Correspondent
Israeli Broadcasting Authority (Jerusalem)

Nine years ago I was at the Club Mediterranean in northern Israel. To enhance the social life, visitors at these clubs are not allowed to listen to radios or watch television while they are there. During my stay, however, rumor spread that there had been some PLO terrorist activity in a village somewhere in northern Israel. I don't know how the rumor started. Maybe somebody cheated and listened to a radio. I must admit that I wasn't too honest either: I had a radio in my luggage which, until that point, I had been faithful and I had not listened to it. But upon hearing the rumor, I unpacked my transistor and took it to the beach. People gathered around me and we listened to the play-by-play broadcast from the village where the activity was taking place. Luckily enough, the event ended without many casualties. After hearing the commentary and analysis on the radio, the people who had been listening turned to me and asked "So what really happened?" I said, "Why do you expect me to know?" "Because you are a journalist. You should know the inside story," they replied. "But I'm here with you on the beach," I said. I realized, however, that the incident was an illustration of the mystique surrounding journalism and the impact we journalists have on public opinion.

We should always remember that whenever we describe or comment on a terrorist event, there are people who are listening to us, taking us very seriously. We should take events--especially terrorist events which have such a huge impact on people's lives--very seriously ourselves and think before we broadcast or write. With respect to the role of the person covering a terrorist event while it is occurring in Israel, military censorship will have some effect on the journalist's report. The term "military censorship" sounds terrible for some people, but the guidelines governing terrorist activities and initiatives are fairly liberal, stating that the press can cover anything except for operational activities. As a result, journalists have established a modus vivendi which involves the military authorities.

Dr. Dieter Kronzucker
Washington Correspondent
ZDF German Television (Channel 2)

In West Germany, terrorism is considered by many as a historical episode that started in the 70's and fizzled out in the 80's. Why did it begin and then end? Many believe that it started in Latin America in 1970 when a German ambassador was taken hostage and killed in Guatemala. The incident received a great deal of press coverage in Germany. Many journalists uttered sympathy with the socio-economic situation in Guatemala, indicating that this was a means to fight a brutal dictatorship and that the German Ambassador accidentally became part of that fight.

A year later a German ambassador was taken hostage in Brazil. This situation triggered mixed reactions on the part of the German press, with some lamenting the liberal stance of the German government and others being sympathetic toward the rebels.

One of the reasons why we heard of the Baader-Meinhof group and other terrorists in Germany is that there was a kind of adoration for the guerrilla in Latin America. For example, Che Guevara became a German national hero. This meant that the rudimentary political basis of the Baader-Meinhof group was focused on the theories used by Latin American guerrillas. The German terrorist thus turned to violent means--killings and kidnappings of German officials, managers and so on. The German government took a liberal stance and in most cases, the conditions of the kidnappers were fulfilled. In one case, the guerrilla even made press coverage part of the bargain, i.e., the exchange of the prisoners held hostage by the Baader-Meinhof group had to be shown on both television networks live. This changed a lot of the minds of my fellow colleagues. It was the start of cooperation between the government and many journalists, especially in the television media. After this turning point in journalism, strangely enough, terrorism declined. Many people became fed up with the tactics of violent terrorist groups because they were not as successful as they were in the beginning and because the police became much more effective. The German government thus came to an agreement regarding the response to terrorism. This pact between press and government, which is very unusual, was part of fighting the guerrillas.

QUESTIONS FROM THE AUDIENCE

Sarah Midgley
The Media Institute

Mr. Kital, you mentioned that while you were at the Club Med, you decided to listen to your radio to learn about the violence in northern Israel. In light of that decision, what is your reaction to Mr. Ashford's proposal to delay reporting on terrorist activities?

Shalom Kital

I do not accept Mr. Ashford's premise. In Israel, as I said, for every terrorist activity that occurs, we journalists have our modus vivendi with the military authorities and, unfortunately, a lot of experience with this method. So the public knows how we operate. Israel's press is a free and aggressive press in which a lot of criticism is aimed at the government. We want to be at the scene of the action to collect evidence and then to pose questions to the government such as "Have you done everything you possibly can to rescue the hostages?" "Is it a good and right and just policy to refrain from negotiating with the terrorists for the hostages?"

Nicholas Ashford

I did not mean to imply that the news of a terrorist incident should in itself be delayed; I do not think we can delay the news of such an incident. What I was suggesting was that the operational details of dealing with the incident should be withheld.

John McLaughlin

In other words, the revelations of the press might defeat the operations of the police?

Nicholas Ashford

Yes, exactly.

John McLaughlin

This happened very graphically in New York. The police were trying to apprehend some terrorists and the activities of the police could be seen by a person in a nearby apartment. The press located that person and put him on the air to recite what the police were doing, thus providing a blow-by-blow outline to the terrorists of where the police were.

Diego Asencio

Every time the terrorists reached an impasse during the seige on the Dominican Mission in 1978, they relied on their radios to pick up any and all information to determine what the impact had been on the outside. I would think that any crisis manager in such a situation would avoid providing terrorists with this kind of information.

John McLaughlin

So you favor a temporary blackout during these periods?

Diego Asencio

I have absolutely no objection to broadcasts informing the public of the occurrence of a terrorist incident and reporting on local reactions. However, I would think that it is standard in any barricade situation to exclude terrorists from any information on police operations.

John McLaughlin

Did anyone notice different viewpoints in the presentations by Dr. Kronzucker and Mr. DeMedici? Mr. DeMedici takes the position that journalists are tools of politicians. Dr. Kronzucker says that politicians are instrumentalized, i.e., journalists are entering their own environment of reporting news with an ideology, which we all have, and with a set of preconceptions, which we all have. By assigning, either consciously or unconsciously, a celebrity status to terrorists, the journalist thus uses the politician or the terrorist to advance his own beliefs.

Marino de Medici

I consider that journalists are politicians. In Italy we are political participants. We are protagonists. It is obvious that we play upon ideological and political conditions. There has been an agreement among many of the media not to give publicity to terrorists. Unfortunately, this could not be implemented 100%. And as long as somebody does not play by the rules, the intentions are obviously defeated. It is unfortunate, but it is a fact of free press. The pact between the authorities and the media in other countries to suppress certain information is definitely out of place in Italy. We cannot even conceive of it. The Italian press is a very vociferous vehicle of ideas, ideologies and political convictions, and it would be impossible to get that kind of consensus. I say "unfortunately," but look at the reverse side of the coin: the Italian press is free.

John McLaughlin

Does the panel agree that the media should help criminal justice processes and that justice officials should turn to the media for professional assistance in handling terrorist incidences and limiting their repercussions?

Dieter Kronzucker

You put forth two propositions: one was aiding; the other was consulting. I would differentiate between the two. The very moment a journalist can solve or help to solve a crime, he should take part in government action. But the very moment the government comes to the journalist to achieve its rules and regulations, then I say no.

John McLaughlin

Do the others maintain that the press should not get into the business of helping law enforcement officials? I find it strange, for example, that BBC says "BBC's credibility depends much more on impartiality than on balance. Our responsibility lies as much in reflecting the significance of the voices of the people <u>including subversion</u> as in sustaining institutions of democracy not wholly accepted." This seems to mean that terrorists are voices of the people and that it is all right to reflect their propaganda because those terrorists do not wholly accept the institutions of democracy. Do you have any comment on that, Mr. Ashford?

Nicholas Ashford

I am not employed by BBC, but I see the point which they are making. In a sense, it is the same point I was making at the beginning. One must try to distinguish whether somebody is attempting to present a genuine political point of view. Most terrorist organizations do have political objectives, and I think it is important that these objectives be heard, even if they are ultimately rejected.

John McLaughlin

We had a particularly vile situation in the U.S. in Jacksonville, Alabama, where a person set himself on fire. The TV camera people did not try to stop the blaze until it was well under way. It has been argued by some press people that that is not their role. Analogously to a terrorist situation, one could argue that if you are a journalist, you are a journalist first and a citizen second rather than vice versa. Doesn't this go to the heart of the whole problem?

Yonah Alexander

I cannot speak for journalists because I am not a working journalist. I am merely an observer. It seems to me that in many situations the human element comes first...that if there is an opportunity to assist the law enforcement authorities to save lives then journalists have to collaborate. Journalism, like any other profession, is secondary to saving lives. If we return to the roles and responsibilities of the media, I think the simplest approach in a democracy would be to bring together the law enforcement officials and the media to find some way to collaborate in order to do their job properly.

Ali Birand

I think Nicholas Ashford's comments point to the main problem in making the distinctions between the terrorist and the freedom fighter. Who is going to decide? Are we the judges? The press is not elected, but we criticize everything and we judge--because of our ideological approaches or whatever--and we say, "Yes, this is a freedom fighter. This is good." So your stories start becoming more sympathetic. But if the press, once and for all, could stop helping the terrorists, then maybe we could have a much better world.

Nicholas Ashford

I think that we are basically in agreement on this point regarding the thin edge between ideology and politics on one side and brutal acts of terrorism on the other side. It is a constant problem of where the freedom fighter becomes a terrorist. This dilemma is summed up in our own case. The British press generally regard and refer to the IRA as terrorists. We tend to regard the PLO as guerrillas, and SWAPO is perceived as being in the middle. But the IRA affects us directly and the PLO does not.

Professor John Norton Moore
Center for Law and National Security
University of Virginia

With regard to the issue of how to determine whether someone is a freedom fighter or a terrorist, the international law tradition provides real insight into this fundamental moral element at issue. Let's take major conflict--not low-level violence, but war between nations-- and posit the clearest conceivable setting: a democratic government attacked ruthlessly and suddenly by a totalitarian regime bent on taking over the country. In the ensuing war, there are a variety of laws of war that apply to both sides, even though in that particular setting the morality of the democratic government seeking to preserve its own self-determination is as clear and ringing as one could possibly imagine. There are a variety of rules, however, that say you do not attack civilian populations.

The issue here is precisely the same as in low-level violence. Our concern is with the question of applying a set of human rights to low-level violence situations precisely as if the perpetrators had been struggling for the last hundred years to achieve their aims in major conflict. The moral point is to get <u>away</u> from questioning the justice of the cause, one way or the other. That is not the issue of low-level violence any more than it is the issue for settings of major conflict. The point on which the press and everyone else needs to focus is that there are certain kinds of acts of violence that are simply beyond the pale. And they happen to be the kind of acts in which terrorists are engaged today. <u>That</u> is where we need to have a clear understanding of what is really at stake.

Nicholas Ashford

This is what makes terrorism so insidious. Everybody is a target. Thus it is impossible to protect potential targets. How can we go about protecting individual people? The terrorist will not discriminate among targets. They will kill aimlessly.

Audience member

I have listened very carefully to what the War and Peace Committee has been discussing for nine months and one particular catchword was "deterrence." What is this deterrence? Following your words, Mr. Moore, deterrence has no place in the model.

John Norton Moore

I don't know that what was said had anything to do with deterrence. I strongly support deterrence as a way to avoid major conflict. The question is whether, in conflict settings, there ought to be a variety of human rights and standards that govern the kinds of targets that one has available in that kind of setting. The answer, it seems, is affected by whether we establish major conflict settings as a fundamental human rights issue. For example, if Lieutenant Calley goes out in the middle of a conflict and shoots innocent civilians, he is a war criminal. He is tried. Now in a low-level violence setting, if an Armenian terrorist attacks a diplomat, then it is a human rights violation, quite apart from the justice of the cause.

A few years ago I participated in the U.S. Convention to Prevent the Spread of Terrorism in the aftermath of the Munich massacre. The Convention was extremely neutral on the question of whether one had the right to revolt. We focused on "advance in conflict matter" to prevent the spread of civil violence abroad, i.e. to say that it is illegal to take your own internal conflict--whatever it may be--and fight it on the territory of another country. What kind of response did we get when we presented that to the United Nations? It was exactly what we hear everywhere. We must study the causes of terrorism first. The point is that of course there are political underpinnings to terrorism. Our task is to separate the activities which are simply beyond the pale. Attacks on diplomats are. Attacks on civilian populations are.

John McLaughlin

Mr. Moore, today's discussion is focused on the intersection between journalists and terrorists. Linking your comments to the subject at hand, are you saying that there is no neutral "no man's land" or that there should be none, as far as journalism is concerned, when terrorism is at play? Is it a journalist's responsibility not to make excuses for terrorism emanating from the civil unrest in a country which is caused by corruption, or abuse of power, or brutality behind the scenes, or unfair harrassment? Are you saying that those factors are really irrelevant when a terrorist incident is at hand, because a new set of criteria then come into play, requiring the journalist--because he is a human being first--to recognize the vile and hideous nature of the act itself? Is that what you are saying?

John Norton Moore

I would be sympathetic with a lot of those points. I am not trying to suggest for a moment, however, that in the interplay of press and the government, the political causes are not going to come out. What I am saying is that it is very important for us to understand what is really wrong with terrorism in a moral sense and why it is really wrong in a conflict management setting in which we are (1) concerned as moral human beings, and (2) concerned in terms of overall world order principles.

Audience member

We are getting to a point of semantics. Is a PLO member who shoots an Israeli soldier on the West Bank a terrorist? On the other hand, is the man who threatened to blow up the Washington Monument a protester? When the word "terrorist" is used to cover everything, it loses its fear value.

John McLaughlin

There is no such thing as a tabula rasa when the press approaches a situation. Journalists have their own preconceptions. When we hear about the Somocistas fighting in Honduras and in Nicaragua, those counter-revolutionaries are clearly being treated differently than the guerillas fighting in El Salvador.

We have discovered or touched upon the full range of issues in this discussion. It is my pleasure to introduce William Claire, who is going to conclude our session.

William Claire
Director, Washington Office
State University of New York

I have decided to make my concluding remarks by not concluding. It would be impossible and foolhardy to summarize the variety of this conference. On behalf of the State University of New York and The Media Institute, I hope that what has transpired here has been a genuine learning experience for all of you.

Appendix: Statistical Overview of Terrorist Incidents*

Type of Victim of International Terrorist Incidents

	1982	1983
Total	791	898
Government Officials	30	62
Diplomats	413	455
Military	89	127
Business	145	101
Private parties, tourists	29	97
Other	85	56

Category of International Terrorist Incidents

	1982	1983
Total	791	898
Kidnapping	31	41
Barricade	18	35
Bombing	335	314
Armed attack	7	24
Hijacking	30	46
Threats, hoax	263	336
Sniping	22	13
Other	39	48

*Statistics provided by the U.S. Department of State Office for Combatting Terrorism

Geographic Distribution of International Terrorist Incidents

	1982	1983
Total	791	898
North America	61	57
Latin America	172	207
Western Europe	340	311
USSR/Eastern Europe	16	11
Sub-Saharan Africa	18	39
Mideast and North Africa	122	193
Asia/other	62	80

Geographic Distribution of International Terrorist Incidents, 1981, by Category

Type of Event	North America	Latin America	Western Europe	U.S.S.R./ Eastern Europe	Sub-Saharan Africa
Kidnapping	0	10	6	0	1
Barricade-hostage	3	13	12	0	1
Bombing[a]	12	25	89	1	9
Armed Attack	0	7	2	0	1
Hijacking[b]	4	9	2	8	1
Assassination[c]	2	7	30	4	3
Sabotage	0	0	1	0	0
Exotic pollution	0	1	0	0	0
Subtotal	21	72	142	13	16
Bombing (minor)	12	33	52	2	6
Threat	15	18	15	6	6
Theft, break-in	1	4	5	0	0
Hoax	34	17	18	3	1
Other[d]	5	12	17	1	3
Subtotal	67	84	107	12	16
TOTAL	88	156	249	25	32

Type of Event	Middle East/ North Africa	Asia	Pacific	Unknown	Total
Kidnapping	5	0	0	0	22
Barricade-hostage	3	0	0	0	32
Bombing[a]	33	1	0	0	170
Armed attack	15	0	0	0	25
Hijacking[b]	3	5	0	0	32
Assassination[c]	20	3	1	0	70
Sabotage	0	0	0	0	1
Exotic pollution	0	0	0	0	1
Subtotal	79	9	1	0	353
Bombing	13	4	0	0	122
Threat	7	6	0	0	73
Theft, break-in	2	1	0	0	13
Hoax	6	5	1	0	85
Other[d]	22	2	0	1	63
Subtotal	50	18	1	1	356
TOTAL	129	27	2	1	709

[a] Bombings where damage or casualties occurred, or where a group claimed responsibility.
[b] Hijackings of air, sea, or land transport.
[c] Includes assassination or attempt to assassinate where the victim was preselected by name.
[d] Includes conspiracy and other actions such as sniping, shootout with police, and arms smuggling.

HV 6431 .T463

DATE DUE			